#MyUglyTruth: The Rhythm of My Life Through Poetry, Writings & Nonsense

Complex Simplicity

BookLeaf Publishing

India | USA | UK

Presentation by *BookLeaf Publishing*

Web: www.bookleafpub.com

E-mail: info@bookleafpub.com

ISBN: 978-93-5744-383-8

First edition 2022

DEDICATION

To Me.

To being Me Unapologetically!!

ACKNOWLEDGEMENT

Mom
Sister
Me

PREFACE

Balance is an illusion, everything is held
together by something....

\- CMPLX
SMPLCTY

I Saw Her From Afar

I saw her from afar,
Well I didn't really see HER,
I saw a FORM of her
She stared at me with deep pain in her eyes
She needed my help.
I tried reaching out but, couldn't move
Paralyzed by confusion and fear.
Tried reflecting love through my eyes
But, I didn't know how.
My mouth tried to utter reassuring words
Nothing was heard.
For I only speak lies.
Her very being began to disappear before my
eyes.
No more!
So....
I stayed
That was my contribution to her.
Staying.
1 tear fell, then 2
They didn't stop.
I watched as she choked on my tears,
Paralyzed.
She would be drowning soon
I can't swim.

But, I stayed.
I stayed until her last breath
No touch.
No words.
Just me.
Staying.
I think that's....Love
I've never stayed before, she has me captivated.
There was nothing else I could do.
So, I cried too!
No one else, just me and you
You and I.
We cried.
Then....
She died.
I hurt inside.
For the one that perished,
Was a form....of me
I saw her from afar.

Pieces Of Me

Tearing away pieces of me
Ripped.
Only way to soothe the pain is:
Pain for Pain.
It hurts so good!
Wishing for control,
Denied.
Desire for blood and pain are overwhelming
I'm Weak.
Digging into my flesh
Showing no remorse
Salivating.
Eyes closed.
Jaws Clenched.
Surrendering to the other me
For I AM NOT myself when I indulge
Good skin bad skin
Dead skin live skin
Dying flesh.
This is my de-stress,
Making myself hurt.
It hurts.
Loving only parts of me
No.
Pretending to Love.... Me

Parts of me look worse than my conditions
But, it's ok.
In the morning,
My skin would have healed
From the tearing and the blood,
From the trauma.
My scars can be hidden with nice threads
But, what remains is,
The reason for my indulgence in self
destruction....and the pain.
Pain demands to be felt.
So, I feel it.
It's ok with me.
But, I am physically destroyed.
Sometimes my exterior matches my interior,
Perfectly.

Pastor Predator

Walking the street searching for answers
Tears falling down my face.
Not understanding my place in this world.
Half way down to my left was a man in a truck
Not sure what I thought probably WTF
But, he called me over...
I was searching for something so I listened
Had no idea the game he was running was
recruiting.
He handed me a track and prayed with me
Tears in our eyes I felt God was moving
Our session was over you stood up to bid me
goodbye
Our eyes were barely dry
Your body didn't lie
You were standing at attention
Abort Mission!!
I ignored the first warning sign
Not really understanding that you crossed a thin
line
See you were a grown man
You knew the boy in you had other plans
When you felt yourself rising to the wrong
occasion

You had the choice to stay seated, hold your
composure, let me make it
But, instead you denounced your title
Allowed the dog in you to surface, you attacked
with no chance of survival.....
No wait
You used me as your own bait
Took me to the church that same day
I was excited about re-dedicating my life
anyway
So I ignored the fact that we were alone
A pastor and a woman with only God to witness
felt a little wrong
The second warning sign is in full effect
I cleared my mind and got undressed
My mom would be proud to know I did this on
my own
Can't wait to talk to her about it when she gets
home
IF....I get home
Idk but here I go
Stepped into the water and it was cold
I think you did that intentionally
Just to see the reaction to my body
A prayer fell from your lips
As I grabbed my nose and you held my wrist
I slid into the water
You pulled me up
I am a new creature

You are the same one
You took a picture
Its the only one you have of me for sure
I hope you enjoyed it sick motherfucker
Or was I the sick one?
I appreciated your kind gesture
You made sure I was good
Took me back home, checked on me a day or
two later like a good pastor should
You knocked on the door and I let you in
We didn't stay long we just talked a little bit
You wanted to take me to lunch, I was hungry so
I allowed it
Taco Bell Church Talk, it was legit
Didn't take me home right away
We went to the park to "talk" and "play"
Yeah, that part got a little crazy
What in God's name was wrong with me that
day?
You treated me like a child playing hide and go
seek
I was 23
You were looking for someone younger than me,
but I took the bait
We walked the trail and talked about the things
we saw
We crossed a bridge he held me from behind
I have no idea what was going through my mind
That threw me off

I pulled away or at least I tried
All I remember after that is his smile
Maybe he was lonely
Maybe he needed a friend
I sacrificed myself so I could be that
Not sure how to feel
But, that's the third warning sign
And I'm still blind
Come on lets keep it real
I think he felt the awkward vibes
I was ready to go home so I asked for a ride
Idk how much time lapsed but he came around
again
Little did I know this would be the end
The night before he came back again
I wrote something to share with him
This is crazy, let me tell you what happened
He wanted to watch a movie in his truck
We picked up Taco Bell again and parked
He parked in a public place where people could
see in
He asked me if I had seen this movie I said no so
he played it
I was shocked by the content
A pastor wouldn't choose this
Dirty humor, foul language and he loved it
Maybe its ok, but, if my mom found out she
would trip
Things happened so fast after that

The movie wasn't even over before he leaned
back
I remember people passing by
Embarrassed and confused as he rubbed my
thigh
It didn't take him long to want more as he
struggled to get inside
I wouldn't allow him to but he tried
He grabbed my hand
And rubbed the bulge in his pants
I thought he was done because I saw a wet stain
I felt sick and wanted to get rid of the aching
pain
I guess he had no interest in the poem I wrote
Belt undone, pants unzipped
His hand on my neck, he wants to feel my lips
He never did
My hands did the work
I couldn't believe this
Had the audacity to apologize for this shit
You said a prayer and asked for forgiveness
I wasn't mad, I understood
Regardless of our title we all do things we
shouldn't
I was 23

I could have ran....
Why didn't I run?
Maybe I was lonely
Maybe I needed a friend
Maybe, just maybe.

The Nightmare Asthma Attack from Hell

Woke up in cold sweat
From a nightmare that found me
Fear represented by the darkness that surrounds
me
Breathe.
Chest tight, head swimming
 My lungs aren't expanding
I place my feet on the floor
Grip my knees for support
Breathe.
There's no air for my lungs to receive
It burns so badly
I dont know how long Ive been struggling
Sit up straight
And pray
Fearing the unknown...
Am I going to take my last breath today?
I'm not going out like this...
FIGHT.
Just one more breath and I'll be alright
In through your nose out through you mouth
Hands above your head
Pray the devils out
Pain in my chest

Pain in my head
Mom in the next room sleeping peacefully in her
bed
Come on, you got this!
Breathe.
Everyone is counting on you, you cant leave yet
Inhale.
Exhale.
Violently trying to breathe
Heart racing
Anxiously looking around for some relief
But there's only darkness to see
Shoulders bent, prayers spent
I'm giving up this fight
Exhaustion kicks in
There's nothing else to do
Nothing left to prove
It's inevitable, I'm going to lose
I prepare myself for my last breath
As I try to utter the words 'Mom, help'
Vision becomes mental
Darkness becomes visual
My life becomes a movie
I am overcome with defeat
My past consumes me
God knows I didn't want to go out like this
Knock, Knock
Who could this be?
I have no strength and Mom is sleep

I have to get to the door
Breathe.
I muster up the strength and fall to the floor
The coolness from the hard wood floors shoots
through my body like electricity
Deep breath.
It gives me energy
Slithering slowly, each shallow breath is a gift
Knock, Knock
No breath to breathe
No thoughts to think
I'm totally done, it's over for me
Mom, I love you keep your head up.
Sis, don't miss what life has to offer you.
To everyone I've loved and that has loved me
I still do.
No worries
My back against the wall
Body completely sore
I extend my arm and unlock the door
My visitor is impatient, they want in now
The door flies open and hits the wall
POW!!
I'm scared awake
Didn't know I had stopped breathing
As I look up I see a dark figure, no face
He grabs my neck, and elevates me from my
space

I'm thrown to the floor as Death takes my place
Mom, you awake?

I Feel This. I Feel That.

I feel this, I feel that
Hurting everywhere, hurting everyone
Feeling accepted, feeling shunned
I'm the disease and I'm the cure
No matter what, they feel secure
I feel that.
But, feel this....
I'm drained
Trying to make everything work is leaving them
pained
Them?
Yes, them....
Them that love you
Them that need you
Them that want what's best for you
I feel that.
But, what's best for you?
What's best for me?
Feel this,
How does someone else know what's best, for
you?
How do you teach yourself to not care?
They expect you to be there
You know that they are all you have

But, you want to move on
Live your life on your own
You just can't
Them....
They....
Her....
She's all I have
They, are all I have
I can't let them go
No regrets
Just secrets untold
I feel this.
I feel that.

Broken

My life is but shattered glass amongst thorns and though I can't fly above the mess to pick up the pieces, nor am I willing for someone else to hurt on my account, I must allow these thorns to break my skin, and I must allow the blood to spill out as the weight of my shattered dreams, and broken heart slip deeper between these thorns. I must collect all of these shards, to place at the feet of my creator so that I may heal and try it once again. You see, I can't do it myself, because through the pain of a broken heart, ripped feet, shredded knees and tears I am bound to make a bigger mess. I only have the strength to collapse at the feet of my Father with pieces. He awarded me whole… but, I only bring Him back pieces. He works tirelessly to rebuild ME….stronger, as I lay in agony I think there is no pain worse than this. I can't move, my body is swollen, I've lost too much blood and my voice is fading from screaming. "Rest" He says…as I lay in agony of my consequences, my spirit was quickened. Weeping may endure for a night, BUT JOY comes in the morning. My eyes closed, my mind calm, my body numb, I REST as He continued to rebuild…ME.

Love Lingers

Two black faces in the dark
Secrets whispered
An unspoken depth
Love lingers
Desire burns between them
Naked bodies yearning
Uniformed thoughts hidden
Love lingers
Anxiousness hurts
Blind eyes searching for more
I see you
But where are you?
I feel you
Between naked bodies
We can't touch
So close yet so far
Love lingers
Words can not escape our mouths
For our voices are mute
No one is here but us
We share this empty space
Our desires are much bigger than our wants
But here we are
Two faces in the dark
Where love lingers

And uniformed thoughts
This is what focus feels like
Bound by your own selfishness
Love lingers
....and love awaits

Relationship Thoughts

Nestled comfortably in my bed
Awaiting our next memory
Wondering if still hear me in your head
Or if you just want me physically
Not sexually....
But physically
No touching
Just watching
This is me thinking
What would it feel like to be blind with you?
Would your words paint a picture of past
visions?
Or would my stubbornness leave me in
darkness?
What if I could no longer walk?
Would you pick me up every morning,
Lay me down every night?
Would you hold me tight,
Scare away the fright?
What would you do if I couldn't speak?
Could you be my words and speak for me?
When you look into my eyes would you know
what I was feeling?

Would you go out of your way to take me places
we used to frequent, even if it was hard for you?
Or would you leave me to start something new
and less stressful with someone else?
Welcome to my relationship thoughts...
Welcome to my relationship.
Thoughts?

Lying

Lying in these sheets
Lying in the streets
Trust doesn't exist
Love missed my heart
Anger keeps me warm
Comfort lies to me

From Lying in these sheets
To lying in the streets
It never ends
Time is timeless
It only lives when we
Stop breathing
My eyes tell it all
My brain makes me fall
Trying not to recall
When I broke your heart
We were working on us
I was hooking up

Lying in these sheets
Ling in these streets
My past paid me a visit
I allowed myself to smile

While convincing me to, 'go the extra mile'

Lying in these sheets
And lying in these streets
Wash. Rinse. Repeat.
Hurt and pain goes around
like a washing machine
Stop the cycle.

Happiness

Happiness is an illusion
As is everything
Nothing is as it seems
But to someone who has it,
Happiness is everything.
It is not.
Happiness fades
As does everything
So if we can't bank on happiness
What do we bank on
Ourselves?!
Ha.
Or is it that I just can't trust myself?
Happiness for me, is darkness
I trust darkness
Because light is only an illusion
As is Happiness
You can find me in the dark,
Happy.
Happiness is an illusion
As is everything.

Letter To Him

Hey
It's your daughter, one of three.

The first time I met you, you were in a run down house on a cot with some lady eating peanut butter and honey out of a jar. Mom and I bought you groceries.

Second time I met you Mom let you stay with her after she kicked me out, I am just realizing this. I was so confused as to why I had to leave AGAIN. Yes, AGAIN. I was separated from Mom Sis and
Stepdad, wasn't sure why until I asked Mom THIS year, 2021. Do you know what the answer was to my question? My grandmother told My Mom that I was better off with her than to hang around my stepdad because stepdads don't treat their stepkids right. Ok. I'll leave it alone.

Third time I met you Mom and I were in San Antonio at church, you came and got me I was so excited. I was young but I remember you bought me a pack of gum at the gas station. You also introduced me to my sister who was

younger than I was who had four kids. She did a
great job by the way! Anywho

The fourth time I saw you, you gave me $100
and alcohol. We drank... And drank more.

The fifth time I saw you I bought you a care
package and you cried.
Why did you cry?
I should have asked you.

Now, you have grown. Im not sure when you did
the work but it seems as if you are now really
into God. I'm proud of you.

You still have a ways to go, but I'm proud
nonetheless. Keep going. I love you.

Weeds Of Protection

I am but a wilted flower in a field of weeds
Weeds wave in the wind but i crumble
My parched petals are blown in every direction
As the weeds wave in the wind
The wind blows all of me away from my roots
My roots
My stem
Planted firmly
Clouds roll in
Rain falls
Sun shines
Months pass
I am recreated
The weeds never stopped growing
They have covered and protected me during my
rebirth
They are tall and nourished as ever
I the flower am stunted
But I shall grow again
Until the wind blows my malnourished petals
again

I Am Black

If i were white
I wouldn't understand but id try
If i were white
I wouldn't be the problem but id still cry
If i were white
I'd use my power the right way
Equality for all black brown yellow trans
straight or gay
If i were white
I'd work hard to see through other's eyes
If i were white
My white friends would have common sense
They would respect and honor all who were
different
If i were white
I wouldn't have to worry about cops trying to kill
or fight....
Me.
But id fight for my neighbors that didn't look
like me
Wrong is wrong
Right is right
If i were white.
But im not white
I have so much beautiful melanin in my skin
That Angelou, King, X and Mandela are my kin

I am black with strength and courage mixed in
I am black so i work harder to understand what's
within
If I were white jealousy would set in
Yet i am black with too much pride
to hide
Grab my coattail let me take you for a ride
Through my history, boldness, courage and
strength
My story will make you cringe
But that's why I'm black with no regrets & no
revenge to get
But yet
A better stronger version of me you won't forget
Living through strength with courage
 I smile
I help
I pray
I love
I stand strong
Because I am black
If I were white
I'd be scared of OUR fight
Yet I am black and that is my right

Check-In

Tears filling my eyes
Throat swelling fast
Heart beating crazy
Just walking to the door made me hurt
Why am I here?
Quick turn around go back before it's too late
It's already too late that's why you are here
If you would've checked in with yourself
You wouldn't need to check in here
It's your fault
You are responsible for you, no one else
How do you feel?
Scared. Very scared.
I just need help no matter how it feels
The psychiatric hospital isn't for the weak
And here I am, at my weakest
Life throwing curve balls I can't catch
My hands tied behind my back
Mental HEALth
Check-In
Are you ok?
No I am not.
Ok, check-in!
Anger swells up inside of me
What little love I had for me was gone

Hate crept in like a new dawn
Tears challenged my tear ducts
I'm tired.
Here we are voluntarily.
I'm here.
Waiting...
Nice people, maybe it's not so bad
Paper after paper with my name in wet ink
More waiting...
A few Lies here and there...
Waiting...
Here we go.
Bye shoestrings
Bye belt
Bye belongings
Bye world.
I jump as the double doors slam behind me
I want to go home
Where is home?
I don't know.
Here maybe?
For now.
Day 1&2 are filled with tears and regret
Day 3-8 are riddled with routines, laughter,
creativity, longing and communication and
GROWTH.
I grew.
I miss it.
I should check-in more often.

Her

Laying next to you seems surreal
Holding you takes me to another world
Loving you gets me high
Looking into your eyes makes my soul cry
They are tears of joy & excitement
I can't believe we are here in this moment
Your smile makes my heart beat
Your body rewards me like a treat
Your soul is a part of me
With you I can just be
Sharing life and space together
Makes me feel connected without pressure
When I'm with you, you keep me calm
I feel protected and loved like the 23rd Psalm
Keep me here
I want to stay right here
Show me how to love you
I'm willing to learn
I'm ready for forever
Please keep me here forever

Choosing

From Him to Her
Choosing Her not Him
Him choosing me not them
Or is he choosing them as well?
Either way I feel special
Am I supposed to feel this way?
Or am I choosing to feel this?
Why am I choosing to feel, period?
Either way the interest is there
It's too late anyway I'm with her
He's with another
Well I'm with both of them
Two Hers
But, I let one Her go
Maybe I can allow myself to let Him in...
No I can't
It wouldn't hurt to think of Him in my thoughts
It's nice to think
Choosing to think on Him

I Can't Breathe

I can't breathe
Take your knee off my neck
There's no reason for it
I'm human
Like your son, daughter & wife
I'm a real person
I deserve better
I'm fighting for it
All I require is love, honesty and respect
So take your knee off my neck
I'm trying to breathe
Everyone is filming me
Why aren't they getting help?
Keep your apologies
They mean nothing
Do you pray to God on the same knee?
While my sight is going dark
I'm thinking
What about my family...
Are you going to tell them what you did?
It was an accident?
Take your knee off my neck
You still have time to do what's right
I'm getting weaker as the time passes

You're killing me
Your killing us
You must be thinking SOMETHING humane
Because you know what you are doing is insane
Take your knee off my neck
Tell my family I love them
I'm sinking further into deaths grip
YOUR grip
You are not God
Think of me when you hold your wife tonight
You made it back home
Take your knee off my neck
I'm already gone
I can't breathe

#MyUglyTruth

Anxiously searching for answers, from
anywhere, I'm running out of time
Everyone seems to have it together, I can't even
pretend about mine
Where do I go? What do I do? Am I tripping?
I'm fine....
Wishing I could separate myself from this world,
but, I'm intertwined
It's going crazy in here, it feels like Wall Street
All the hustle and bustle on the inside, outside
I'm a zombie
So much going on in my head, I haven't made
time for anything else but, sleep
When I wake up, I hurt. There's pain throughout
my body
Feels like I've been in an explosion and there's
no one around me
Pieces of me are everywhere and I'm slowly
dying
There's no use in me crying
Gotta pick myself up, I'm supposed to keep
trying
If I said this was easy, I'd be lying
Spent most of my life figuring out what "Being
Whole" meant

Too many lies and broken hearts, masked to
appear good....behold it
Behold the fake
Beautiful on the outside, on the inside, ugliness
I'm wanting everyone else's life except mine,
this is foolishness
This Is #MyUglyTruth
Too weak to stay woke
Too tired to remember what I spoke
No energy to fight
Too fearful to take flight
So much stress I'm going blind mentally
My soul is in the dark and I can't see
Spiritually I'm on the dark side
Feeling darkness all around me, I still hide
Reaching for what I thought was mine
But it wasn't, it was theirs, not my time
So far down at the bottom, on my tippy toes and
still can't touch the light
Grabbed my heart and shivered, it was cold as
ice
Melting away with every touch til I lay lifeless,
no life
This is #MyUglyTruth
So stressed I couldn't hold my bodily fluids
Struggling to fit in and blend in, I'm in ruins
"To be or not to be" is the question that I'm
persuing
My mental health unstable

My kind unfavorable
Those people over there, think I'm incapable
The worst part is, I believe them and I'm to
impatient to prove them wrong
I wish I was strong.
I need something to take this pain away
Because, I'm showing my naked self today
I've been higher than the clouds, with no Red
Bull in me
Rolling without wheels, rainbow flinstones, no
vitamins
Dabbing with strangers, no dancing just zombies
I have seen more darkness with my eyes open
then I have with them closed
Written more words than I've ever even spoke
This Is #MyUglyTruth
What would you do?
If the first time love was mentioned outside of
family
Was from the same person who just wanted your
body
You associated sex with love, so you gave it up,
just to feel something inside of you. Love.
Like, your purpose and passion for life wasn't
enough for you
But, it was....you were just too young to
understand what they could and couldn't do for
you
This Is #MyUglyTruth

You had to have pain without a vision, only
empty wishes to get you through
Pretending things are all good and sacrificing
your soul just to look cute
Who am I talking too?
I'm bipolar as hell, no schizophrenic
No structure to my mental emotion but, there's a
method to my madness
"If I got it, Imma spend it" no limits, but, limited
You ain't never been through this?
No Religion but, I grew up in the church
No Fashion Nova, it was fashion over The Word
If you wore the best fit, that determined your
worth
This Is #MyUglyTruth
Pastor had a "weak moment" and chose me to
shatter
It's cool, we are all "Human" our title doesn't
matter
The fragrance of lust lingered in his truck
Grabbing my neck he begged me to show him
love
"No" was my silent answer, so I had to touch
Prayer was next, you asked for forgiveness while
our heads were bowed
What number am I? I wanted to shout out loud
Do you do this often? Are you proud?
What do I do now?

Wondered how I could be so stupid with my
head in the clouds
I won't lie, that seemed way too easy for you
You baptized me, prayed for me and gave me
several reasons to report you
Just like your gifts, your sins will make room for
you
Maybe that's a little harsh but, I make mistakes
too
Making mistakes is what I'm used to
I just pray you don't mention me to God, keep
my name out your mouth
Don't be ashamed, don't hate yourself, I forgive
you
What I won't do is forget, hence, I'm telling
#MyUglyTruth
Some of you may think that this is enough
Telling you about my past is way too much
Well Maybe if you told #YourUglyTruth it
wouldn't be so difficult for you to hear mine
I've hurt more people than I realized
I've been hurt a thousand and ten times
But, that's ok with me
Been through a lot, doesn't mean I can get away
with it
Thought I was good, but, ten years later, Karma
is still a trip
Hurt people, hurt people
It could be an excuse but it's moreso a brand

People feed us and we bite that same hand
We've been doing this for years
Maybe I'm the only one crying regretful tears
I'm definitely not perfect, but, guilty of
becoming my own fears
Filling everyone's cup except mine, only
emptiness remains
I only pray whoever God has for me, is stronger
than my pain
This Is #MyUglyTruth
All of this and I still have no answers
Running around in circles with my brains
scattered
Thought I figured out one thing, then comes a
whole new issue
Wish I had more self control, I just keep getting
triggered
No Alice but, I'm in a Wander-land, just call me
the Mad Hatter
I wander and wander til I can't feel my feet
Me: God where you at? Can you carry me?
God: Nah it's your fault, you walked away from
me
Granted, your love is legit
I guess understanding isn't my language and
freedom isn't free
Much more is expected of me
That much I get, but, why so much?
I'm going through the same thing....

Over and over and over again
What am I missing?
What are you trying to teach me?
I know most of this is my fault, the blame is on
me
Going through life blessed, but, choosing to be
unhappy
I'm not trying to
I just feel as if I'm forced to love you
Trying to find my own way is difficult
I'm being punished for not pushing through
...and following the path that was paved for me
to endure
Idk if I should even be saying this
I'm all alone drowning in my own sins
No answers....
Just scavenger hunts, no clues
This is #MyUglyTruth
Unmasked and naked, I'm unforgiven, because, I
ask not
Knowing that I refuse to change my life for HIM
Knowing that I never finish what I begin
Why should I be forgiven?
I sow pain and suffering and harvest an
unforgiving spirit
So, let me simmer in my sin
I deserve to be alone, that's why, I let no one in
You can't tell me to keep pushing or keep trying,
that's so selfish to me

I didn't ask to be here and neither did you
So, a little understanding is what I expect from you
Though I adore you for staying strong and helping me too
There are quite a few things that I need to work through
This is #MyUglyTruth
I'd rather be in the dark, dark where light can't penetrate
You know a lot of so called Christians won't go there, yeah take me to that place
Take me to where God can't reach
....and you won't preach
Give me fake and fantasy
Anything to get me away from reality
They say change starts with me
With that comes responsibility
I can't even take care of myself
Why would you give me someone else to help?
This is a time for ME to be fixed
To the rest of y'all aren't getting picked
Yes, right now I'm SELFISH, I have to be that first before I'm SELFLESS
This Is #MyUglyTruth
Got all this anger inside of me
Which has me awarding my enemy with an Emmy
For the best attempt at a fatality

'Cause I'm barely breathing
Thought it was my asthma but, the longer I'm
down the value of my life is depreciating
Everyone around me is patiently waiting
They have all invested in me
Whether it was for good or bad
I'm barely alive reflecting back to the battles I've
had
This Is #MyUglyTruth
Who is gonna really suffer when I'm done?
Done with life, and all it's trials and pressures
and being alone
Alone in my head, with no one to witness
This just took a turn for the worst.... I am
finished
This is #TheUglyTruth
This is #MyUglyTruth

Personal Power

A little backstory on me, I was raised most of
my life in a single parent home with my younger
sister. Our Mother raised us. Everything was fine
until it wasn't, the universe decided to shake
things up.
I was sent to live with Grandmother and
Grandfather. There I cleaned, took care of my
grandparents, went to school, had no friends and
when family came for the holidays, I had to save
face. No one knew how broken I was, no one
knew that I missed my family . I felt like my
mom and new step dad were out living their best
life without me while I slaved for grandma and
grandpa. They didn't want me, and that hurt.
No one knew how helpless and broken I felt.
This continued for a while, too long if you asked
me, I would pray that one day my family would
come back for me.
That day came, I was so happy. I knew they
missed me. So they packed me up and we left
from Texas and headed to Arizona. New
adventure, new life.
Fast forward to age 16. We had to leave
Arizona, my Mom wasn't enough for my
stepdad. Mom packed my sister and I up and

we headed back to Texas after 3 years in Arizona. In Texas we would face homelessness, I would get kicked out and forced to live with my aunt, my sister would get sick and I would be broken over and over again into small pieces by life.

⏩ Fast forward again to December 23, 2020 in the middle of a pandemic I found what would be the best representation of Love I have ever witnessed. January 1,2021 we made it official with a promise of never leaving, always communicating, tough love, healing and growth. I was amazed that someone would take the time to water, inspire, prune, encourage and support me. Not only that, but I too, would learn how to reciprocate these actions. My partner gave me a fresh mirror, and allowed me to reflect. I had no idea what was in store for my future.

⏩ Fast Forward to September 1, 2021 my Mom and I stumbled into a conversation. It happened so fast, I had no I what was going on until I felt an intense wave of confidence as I combed over the lessons taught to me by my partner. My partner was created specifically for me, to groom me for moments like these. Words of encouragement, love, healing, forgiveness, understanding and patience rolled of my lips and fell onto my mother's heart. She never knew how I was treated with my grandparents. But, that day September 1, 2021, I found out that she too was treated the same, she was hurt time and time again by her Mother, My father, My sister's father, her sisters her brother….the list goes on. And I'm here for it all. My mother was made aware of her traumas and took her Power back. Even though both grandparents are gone, my mother has a better understanding of what she needs to begin to heal her traumas. I realized that I have the superpower of empowerment

You know know that wave of confidence I told you about?

That was my Personal Power given to me by my partner, the universe and my ability to overcome.

Now, I give it to you.

Be strategic.

Be aware.

Be empowered.

Be the change.